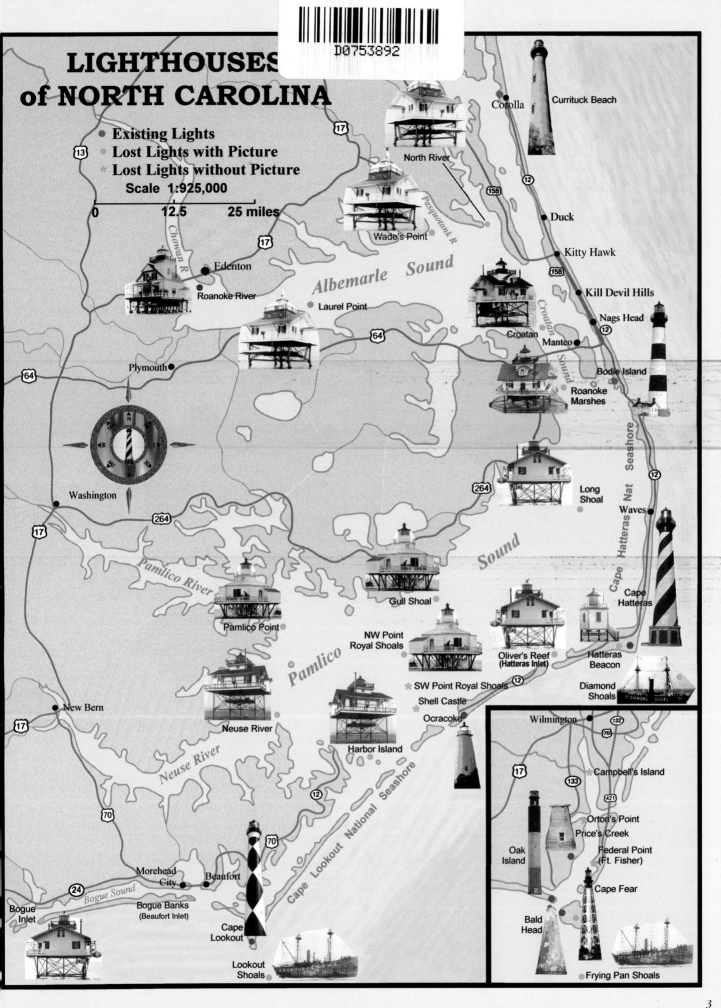

LIGHTHOUSES
of NORTH CAROLINA

- Existing Lights
- Lost Lights with Picture
- * Lost Lights without Picture

Scale 1:925,000

0   12.5   25 miles

Corolla
Currituck Beach

North River

Posquotank R

Chowan R

Edenton
Roanoke River

Wade's Point

158

12

Duck

Kitty Hawk

158

Kill Devil Hills

Albemarle Sound

Laurel Point

64

Croatan

Croatan Sound

Nags Head

12

Manteo

Plymouth

Bodie Island

Roanoke
Marshes

Washington

264

264

Long
Shoal

Cape Hatteras Nat Seashore

12

Waves

Pamlico River

Sound

Pamlico Point

Gull Shoal

Cape
Hatteras

Pamlico

NW Point
Royal Shoals

Oliver's Reef
(Hatteras Inlet)

Hatteras
Beacon

New Bern

Neuse River

* SW Point Royal Shoals

Diamond
Shoals

Shell Castle
*
Ocracoke

Neuse River

Harbor Island

12

Cape Lookout National Seashore

70

Wilmington

132

76

17

Campbell's Island

133

421

Orton's Point
Price's Creek

Oak
Island

Federal Point
(Ft. Fisher)

Morehead
City

Beaufort

70

Cape Fear

24

Bogue Sound

Bogue Banks
(Beaufort Inlet)

Bogue
Inlet

Cape
Lookout

Bald
Head

Lookout
Shoals

Frying Pan Shoals

3

CURRITUCK BEACH LIGHT STATION

(Site established 1873, Light activated 1875)

Visiting a lighthouse can be a rich experience. Every human sense is involved from smelling the ocean breeze to touching time that is locked within the historic fabric of the extant structures. Additionally, there is something for every one: history, architecture, romance, and mystery. The one richer experience, perhaps, is visiting a restored light station. Therefore, walking onto the compound of the Currituck Beach Light Station offers one of the richest lighthouse experiences in North America.

Lighted December 1, 1875, the Currituck Beach Lighthouse was the last tall, coastal light to be built by the U.S. Lighthouse Service along the Outer Banks of North Carolina. With its 1st order Fresnel lens, it shed light on the last dark stretch between Cape Henry and Bodie Island. These lofty lights along the ocean that had 1st order Fresnel lenses were known as "lighthouses of the first order."

As soon as the Civil War ended, the Light-House Board began rebuilding many destroyed southern lights as well as construction of new lights to replace poorly constructed and aging lighthouses. This building plan included new towers along the featureless, shoal-studded North Carolina coast. Initially at Cape Hatteras, second at Bodie Island, and a third was planned at a new site for Currituck Beach. All three were to be based on the successful design first tried at Cape Lookout in 1859. Dexter Stetson, foreman of construction for the Lighthouse Service, supervised the construction of all three new towers.

Similar to Cape Hatteras and a twin to Bodie Island, the architectural plans for the Currituck Beach Light were familiar to Stetson, and perhaps possess the greatest flair of his three towers. Enhancement can be seen in a more spacious oil room, entryway, two brick sidewalks, and an added gem to the light station in the two-story, stick-style (1876) Double Keepers Quarters.

The lighthouse tower is approximately 158 feet to the focal plane, which is the center of the lantern room where light is emitted. Its 1st order Fresnel lens originally carried a "fixed varied revolving flash" nineteen nautical miles out to sea. The characteristic of its unique light emitted a long white beam followed by two eclipses with a red flash in between. The huge 1st order Fresnel lens was turned by a clockwork mechanism driven by a weight that the Keeper wound up about every two to three hours. This flash characteristic gave Currituck Beach its nighttime identity to mariners.

Top left: The beautiful 1st order Fresnel lens, installed in 1875 still does active duty, lighting the horizon each evening.

Bottom left: The Double Keepers Quarters (DKQ) at the Currituck Beach Light Station is undergoing meticulous restoration by its caretakers, Outer Banks Conservationists, Inc. The house has three floors, split down the middle so that each side of the house mirrors the other. One Keeper and his family lived on one side, and the second Keeper and his family occupied the other half of the house. There were only three grand DKQs like this built in the U.S. by the Lighthouse Service, and the one pictured here is the lone survivor today, thanks to restoration. At lower left is one of two cisterns that stored fresh rainwater from eaves on the roof. Rain collected in the eaves and ran down pipes into the cool storage area below ground. There is a cistern on each side of the house that provided the Keepers and their families with fresh water.

Construction began in 1873 when the first of approximately one million bricks were laid in double wall construction, tapering from about five and one-half feet to three at the top of the brick tower. Distinguishing daymarks had already been painted (1873) in black and white "checkers" on Cape Lookout, spirals on Cape Hatteras, and bands on Bodie Island. This allowed Currituck Beach to wear its natural red brick color as its daymark.

When Currituck Beach was built, the quaint Corolla village scene was quiet and sparsely inhabited. The Keepers at Currituck Beach had few visitors who traveled the lonely stretch of sand between the Currituck Sound and the Atlantic Ocean for miles along the barrier island, punctuated by only an occasional scene of a shipwreck or a beached whale. Family life at the lighthouse provided occupation, education, and social life. Reaching Currituck was difficult at best. For those fortunate to have a car, tires were deflated for driving on the beach. It was not until 1984 that a paved road to Duck was completed.

The area was once known as Whale's Head. Legend has it that a large whale washed ashore and according to various accounts, a man walked inside or drove his car into the opened jaws. Likely, mariners conjured up this name because a large dune on the island resembled the shape of a whale.

Today, the Currituck Beach Lighthouse remains an active aid to navigation, warning mariners of the nearby shoals with three seconds of white beam followed by 17 seconds eclipse. Since being automated, the light shines at dusk and goes off at dawn. The Fresnel lens and 1,000 watt light bulbs are maintained by the U. S. Coast Guard.

The light station is nearing complete restoration by Outer Banks Conservationists, Inc. (OBC), a nonprofit organization that maintains the light station under lease agreements from the N.C. Department of Cultural Resources and the U.S. Coast Guard. Visitors can enjoy viewing exhibits that interpret the light station's history, walk around the beautiful compound, and visit the museum/gift shop near the tower. For a modest fee, visitors can also climb the 214 steps and walk onto the catwalk at the gallery level for a panoramic view from sound to sea. The beautiful Whalehead Club, also undergoing restoration, borders the lighthouse property.

To learn more about the Currituck Beach Lighthouse and to help in its preservation, you may want to consider a membership in the Outer Banks Conservationists, Inc., the nonprofit group that has beautifully restored this historic light station. For more details, call 252-453-8152, or write OBC at P.O. Box 970, Manteo, NC 27954.

🐦 Quick notes...

Directions: Take Highway 12 North from 158 in Kitty Hawk to Corolla. Lighthouse is visible from the road on your left. Turn left into the light station's parking area.

- Lighthouse grounds are open, and the lighthouse is open for climbing from 10-6 daily and 10-5 in November.
- Restoration is funded by visitors paying to climb, donations, and sponsorships of Outer Banks Conservationists, Inc.
- There are 214 steps up the spiral staircase.
- The tower measures 162 feet to the top of the roof.
- There are nearly one million bricks in the tower.
- Wall thickness tapers from 5 feet 8 inches to 3 feet at the parapet.
- The present flash characteristic is one white flash every 20 seconds (3 seconds on and 17 seconds off) from a 1st order Fresnel lens, and the beam reaches 19 nautical miles out to sea.
- website: http://www.currituckbeachlight.com or call 252-453-8152.

The Currituck Beach Lighthouse rises gracefully on the light station grounds. It remains unpainted so it can be distinguished from its twin, Bodie Island Lighthouse to the south.

Above: Details of the stick-style architecture over the oil storage entryway have been copied many times by architects designing the "Outer Banks style" for cottages which now line area beaches. Etched in granite over the door to the oil storage entryway is "1871," which marks the year that the present tower's site was established.

At right: A view of the Bodie Island Light Station at dusk is taken from Highway 12. The light station remains virtually free from twenty-first century intrusions, making it a rare photographic opportunity.

BODIE ISLAND LIGHT STATION

Lost tower 1848,
second tower 1859, existing tower 1872

Today's Bodie Island Lighthouse and its Double Keepers Quarters are in one of the most classic settings in America. It is situated midway between the Atlantic Ocean and Pamlico Sound within the protection of the Cape Hatteras National Seashore. As one of the finest lighthouses built by the Light-House Board in 1872, its quiet beauty does not reveal man's struggle to keep a light here.

This graceful lighthouse had two predecessors. The first was built in 1848 about a mile and one-half to the south of Oregon Inlet. Due to lack of foresight on the part of the Fifth Auditor of the Treasury, Stephen Pleasonton, the earliest Bodie Island had no foundation. It took little time for the 54-foot tall white brick tower to sink on one side in the soft, sandy surface. The first tower utilized the Winslow Lewis lighting system consisting of fourteen oil lamps and parabolic reflectors with a red flash panel that was turned by clockwork mechanism. A leaning tower rendered the light even more fitful and difficult for mariners to see at any distance. In 1854 the Light-House Board made some improvements including the installation of a 4th order Fresnel lens, but the failing tower was eventually abandoned.

Again, the one hundred-twenty miles between Cape Henry and Cape Hatteras were dark for mariners. There

remained a great need for a lighthouse at Bodie Island, not only to guide ships along the featureless Outer Banks, but also to warn them to begin a swing away from shore, for danger lay ahead. The ships that were taking advantage of the southern-flowing Virginia Coastal Current had to stay close to shore in order to stay out of the north flowing, warm Gulf Stream twenty miles to the east. Hugging the coast was a dangerous game because of the changing shoals, but moreover, unless these southbound ships began a swing to the east at Bodie Island, they would surely wreck on Hatteras's Diamond Shoals lying in wait forty miles to the south.

The Light-House Board recognized the value of a lighthouse on this site; therefore, a second Bodie Island Lighthouse was built of the finest materials available near the original site in 1858. This time, a secure foundation was laid for the white, eighty-foot tall tower, and it was fitted with a 3rd order Fresnel lens. At last, this site hosted a fine lighthouse. But darker days lay ahead when this youngster was destroyed by Confederates in 1861. The island would remain just another unlighted spot on the Outer Banks until 1872.

After the Civil War, the Light-House Board began repairing the damage from the war as well as constructing new lights. The site for the present Bodie Island Light Station was chosen further north because by 1871, the migration of Oregon Inlet to the south had come within 1,200 feet of the original two sites.

With the experience of building a successful foundation at Cape Hatteras, construction foreman Dexter Stetson opted to use the same plans at Bodie Island. A grid of yellow pine was laid about six feet below ground. On top of the timber

What is the mystique of the ocean?

There is a peace within the strength of the ocean that draws us beside it. As we stand in the water watching the waves break endlessly on shore and feel the pull of the sand as it slips beneath our feet washing back into the water once more, we know that we are one with ageless time.

We sense within us this magic of the coast.

Randy Taylor

grid, kept below the fresh water table to keep it strong, were huge pieces of granite to complete the sturdy foundation for the brick tower. Nearly one million bricks were laid in double-wall construction to a height of 150 feet.

Supplies were lightered in smaller vessels in Pamlico Sound from larger ships to the lighthouse site. Construction materials were brought to a dock equipped with a derrick for offloading materials in what would become known as Stetson's Channel. Wagons were pulled along a tram track to the construction site for Bodie Island.

The soul of the lighthouse is its 1st order Fresnel lens from Barbier & Fenestre of Paris, France; this magnificent light has done double duty for seagoing vessels as well as local traffic on the Pamlico. A typical evening for a Keeper in 1920 would find him climbing the 214 steps with a bucket of coal in one hand and a five-gallon brass can of lamp oil in the other. The coal was for the warming stove in the watchroom, the level below the lantern room, which could become cold as the night wore on. Prior to the 1920s, one Keeper remained on "watch" all night.

In preparation for the night's service, the Keeper would step inside the tall Fresnel lens, fill the lamp's reservoir with oil, and light the wick. After adjusting the flame and making sure it was not smoking or flickering, the Keeper would descend the ladder into the watchroom and prepare to stay the night. The lamp was lit one-half hour before sunset and extinguished the following morning one-half hour after sunrise.

The small Keepers Quarters was the only housing provided up to three Keepers and their families. With no school or church, due to the isolated conditions at Bodie Island, most families stayed only during holidays and summer school vacations. Although another Keepers Quarters was repeatedly requested, the plans never made it off the drawing board.

To modernize the lighthouse, the Lighthouse Service installed an incandescent light that was powered by banks of batteries set in the two workrooms inside the entryway. A flash control motor produced the flash characteristic 2.5 seconds on, 2.5 off, 2.5 on, and 22.5 seconds off. When the light was electrified in 1932, a 1,000-watt bulb with automatic changer was installed.

The Bodie Island Light Station is situated on land surrounded by the Cape Hatteras National Seashore established in 1953. All but 100 feet around the tower has been deeded to the NPS; the Fresnel lens and its light are still maintained by the U.S. Coast Guard. Each year over one hundred thousand visitors travel to see this light. The tower is in need of complete restoration before it can be opened to the public for climbing.

To learn more about North Carolina Lighthouses, you may consider a membership in the Outer Banks Lighthouse Society. It is a nonprofit group which serves as an advocate for the restoration and preservation of North Carolina's Lighthouses. For more information please write to:

OBLHS P.O. Box 1005, Morehead City, NC 28557
and visit their website at:
http://www.outer-banks.com/lighthouse-society.

The Double Keepers House at Bodie Island is the only accommodations ever built at this light station for up to three Keepers and their families. Today, this light station hosts hundreds of thousands of visitors who voice support for its restoration.

(At right) This is the view a Keeper saw each dusk as he stepped into the giant Fresnel lens to light a lamp in the center of the small platform, now occupied by automated, incandescent 1,000-watt electric bulbs. This 1st order Fresnel lens is six feet wide, eleven feet tall, and consists of over 1,000 crown-glass prisms. A Keeper polished this cathedral of glass with soft chamois cloth and fine jeweler's rouge. The utmost care was taken to never damage the prisms. These lenses lit up our field of dreams all around America's shores, taking mariners to faraway places, and guiding them home again.

 Quick Notes...

Directions: From Kitty Hawk take NC 158 south to NC 12 south to the Cape Hatteras National Seashore. About 10 miles south, watch for this tall lighthouse on the right; a sign marks the entrance to the lighthouse. A visitors center and bookstore are housed in the Double Keepers Quarters. As with many salt marsh areas of the Outer Banks, always be prepared with insect repellant.

- There are 214 steps to the lantern room; however, the lighthouse needs restoration, and the tower is not open for climbing.
- The flash characteristic remains 2.5 seconds on, 2.5 off, 2.5 on and 22.5 seconds eclipse per minute.
- Bodie Island originally was spelled "Body" or "Body's" Island. The name appears in all forms possible, including "Bodie's" Island in U.S. Lighthouse Service documents.
- Fresh water was gathered from rain running down eaves on the Keepers Quarters to two cisterns.
- Volunteers from the Outer Banks Lighthouse Society occasionally open the tower's lower portion during the summer.
- Bodie Island's Principal Keeper Vernon Gaskill, Sr. and Assistant Keeper Julian Austin, Sr. were two of the last civilian era Keepers of the U.S. Lighthouse Service. Gaskill transferred to the lighthouse depot in Coinjock, and Austin closed the lighthouse in 1940, ending the Lighthouse Service era at Bodie Island. Like other coastal lights, it became a lookout tower for the Navy during WWII.
- During the 1920's, the Bureau of Lighthouses installed a sensor near the lamp's flame. If something went wrong with the flame, a "call bell" sounded in the Keepers Quarters.

On November 13, 1999, the newly relocated Cape Hatteras Lighthouse once again took up duty over the Graveyard of the Atlantic in a relighting ceremony. This event marked the completion of a bold, monumental move of the lighthouse and all parts of the light station 2,900 feet to the southwest. The Cape Hatteras Lighthouse has torpedoed shots of light across the bows of voyaging vessels since 1870, but beach erosion endangered its long history by threatening to undermine the shallow foundation and take the lighthouse into the sea. Thousands attended the festive occasion, and tribute was expressed in words and music to all who helped to make the relocation a success.

CAPE HATTERAS LIGHT STATION

(1803 and 1870)

The first Cape Hatteras Lighthouse was completed in 1803. Shortly after it was lighted, mariners complained of its dim light, too little warning they said, which did not reach across underwater ridges of shifting sand called Diamond Shoals. These shoals caused shallow waters and were capable of wrecking a ship.

This site marks the battlefield between man and nature. Expert sculptors–wind and water–have shaped the extended hook of this barrier island and the outlying shoals at Cape Hatteras. Offshore currents within the Atlantic Ocean flow in opposite direction: from the north, and closer inshore, are the remnants of a cold water current; flowing from the south is the warm Gulf Stream. The junction of these opposing temperatures frequently produces fog, angry storms, and scouring action by currents that cause sand to shoal.

When ships depended upon wind-driven sails for power, they would often lie off Hatteras, waiting for prevailing winds to carry them out of the area. Avoiding Diamond Shoals put these ships over twelve miles out to sea with no nearby lee, or protective harbor. While waiting for favorable winds, they were often caught in foul weather with winds and waves driving them landward onto Diamond Shoals. While held in the grips of the shoals, the tempest would then tear sails from masts and make splinters of a ship's hull.

One passenger who experienced a frightening trip around Hatteras was Alexander Hamilton, then just a seventeen-year-old lad working on the *Thunderbolt* around 1760. With no light to guide the ship, Hamilton watched as his ship dragged on Diamond Shoals. A fire broke out on board and the ship narrowly escaped sinking.

After 1789, the United States assumed all responsibilities for construction and maintenance of lighthouses under the Department of the Treasury. Alexander Hamilton became Secretary and represented a strong voice for a lighthouse at Cape Hatteras. Born of fire and tempest, the history of the Cape Hatteras Light Station began as "Mr. Hamilton's Light."

As early as 1792, Congress promised to light the North Carolina coast. To begin this effort, four sandy acres were bought for $50.00 from four Jennett orphans. Purchase, deeding, surveying, and procurement of funds for the land took time. Building supplies had to be imported from northern ports, further slowing the project.

Henry Dearborn, builder of the first Hatteras Light, negotiated many problems including an illness, likely malaria, which plagued his workmen. Persevering, Dearborn created a building technique that would become the template for future lighthouse construction. Supplies were brought into a nearby inlet, in this case Hatteras Inlet, and transferred to smaller vessels. The supplies were "lightered" in smaller boats as close to shore as possible and then picked up by workers who got the supplies to shore. Oxen labored to pull the supplies to the lighthouse site along a tramway, much like railroad tracks.

With all the delays, it was not until 1803 that the ninety-foot sandstone tower exhibited a guiding light. Winslow Lewis paired the 1782 Argand lamp with a parabolic reflector system to produce as bright a light as possible. A twelve-foot tall iron frame housed 18 whale oil-fed lamps. It was a tedious job for any Keeper in filling oil reservoirs, cleaning the chimney of each lamp, and polishing the reflectors. However, the sum total of these lights was less than desired, and mariners complained they nearly went aground looking for the Cape Hatteras Light.

Finally, a sweeping effort for improvements began in 1854

for many North Carolina lights. The 1803 Hatteras Light realized a boost in height of fifty feet, raising the focal plane to 140 feet. Additionally, it was fitted with one of the first Fresnel lenses brought to America. The Fresnel lens was a remarkable invention that took one lamp's flame and magnified it into a strong beam of light. Whereas the Winslow Lewis lighting system grouped 18 lamps and parabolic reflectors, the Fresnel lens was the equivalent to approximately 140 of these lamps and reflectors.

For decades, the 1803 tower had fought a constant battle with wind erosion. Its foundation rested on a twenty-foot sand dune that was slowly dwindling, leaving the lighthouse with unsure footing. Following the Civil War, an inspection of the aging tower convinced the Light-House Board that a new lighthouse was in order.

Dexter Stetson, a New England builder, born and resided in the shipbuilding environment of Maine and Massachusetts, was chosen as foreman of construction of the new Cape Hatteras Lighthouse. Its bold plans raised the focal plane to 180 feet, placing the tower's height at 198 feet. Double-brick wall construction allowed it record height. To begin the impressive tower, government plans directed Stetson to drive 601 wood pilings for the foundation. However, Stetson could only drive pilings 9 feet 9 3/4 inches with a steam-powered driver.

Using his shipbuilder's knowledge, Stetson dug a hole six feet deep, rerouted the fresh water that flowed only four feet below the surface of the sand, and laid a three-layered grid of yellow pine in a 46-foot wide area. This timber mat gave the surface upon which the load of the lighthouse would be spread, and when covered in a bath of fresh water, the pine timber would remain steel-strong. On top of the pine timber mat was built an octagonal base of Vermont granite and a tower of one and one-quarter million Virginia bricks. An iron lantern room topped all

this. Bartlett, Robbins, and Company of Baltimore manufacture the ironwork, including the graceful spiral stairs.

Upon its completion, the construction price had inflated to over $150,000. But the tower overshadowed anything on the East Coast and boasted a new 1st order Fresnel lens, then worth approximately $7,000. The new 24-panel, 1870 Fresnel lens turned on chariot wheels; it turned at 1/4 revolutions per minute and exhibited six-2 1/2 second white flashes and six-2 1/2 second eclipses (dark).

The next great improvement for the 1870 tower came in 1913 when a combination of the Fresnel lens and the incandescent oil vapor (IOV) lamp was installed. Akin to today's Coleman lantern, the IOV lamp generated thousands of candlepower for about a quart of oil every two hours.

Beach erosion proved a persistent problem, steadily moving the ocean nearer the lighthouse. Erosion control of various kinds began as early as the 1930s with beach reinforcement. Later in the 1960s, three groins were put in place to combat the disappearing shoreline. A groin is a low-profile steel wall built perpendicular to the shoreline, intended to trap sand as it flows by. The lighthouse was originally built about 1,600 feet from the ocean's edge, but waves came as close as touching the tower after two severe storms in the 1930s. So severe was the erosion problem that the lighthouse was decommissioned and closed in 1936. A steel skeleton tower, equipped with a modern optic, and located in Buxton Woods, took over the job of the Cape Hatteras Light.

By 1953, the Cape Hatteras National Seashore had been established, and the National Park Service worked with the U.S. Coast Guard to reactivate the striped tower. A new era had begun for this light, but erosion would prove a persistent threat.

Below: This aerial view shows the move corridor at the beginning of the relocation of the lighthouse 2,900 linear feet to the southwest. Now located at the right angle turn in the move corridor, the lighthouse is situated 1,600 feet back from the ocean's edge. This is about the same distance from the ocean that the tower was built in 1870.

In 1988, the National Academy of Sciences made an analysis of alternatives for long-term protection for the lighthouse and recommended relocation away from the ocean. The National Park Service then sponsored a one-million dollar restoration of the tower in preparation for a move inland. Until relocation could be accomplished, interim measures were taken to halt erosion, including the landward extension and reinforcement of the southernmost groin and placement of giant sandbags.

In 1997, Congress appropriated $2 million to plan the relocation of the Cape Hatteras Light Station 2,900 feet southwest, once again placing the lighthouse 1,600 feet from the ocean's edge, as it had been when originally built. In 1998, Congress approved the remaining $10 million to make the relocation a reality. International Chimney, Inc. won the move contract, and along with Expert House Movers and a team of engineers, they planned and executed what has been called "the move of the century."

The relocation was accomplished in just twenty-three days. Within days of completing the new foundation under the relocated lighthouse, two hurricanes rolled up the East Coast, causing damage of historic proportions to eastern North Carolina. Fortunately, damage to the lighthouse was limited to smashed windows in the tower.

The lighthouse was relighted in a ceremony November 13, 1999, with tributes in words and music in celebration of the successful move. This announced closure to Phase I of the relocation project.

The history of the Cape Hatteras Lighthouse continues with Phase II bringing further grounds improvements and facilities for interpretation of its long history. Upon opening the lighthouse to the public for climbing on the Friday before Memorial Day 2000, a new chapter in history has begun for this National Historic Landmark.

 Quick Notes...

Directions: From Kitty Hawk take NC 158 south to NC 12 south to the Cape Hatteras National Seashore entrance. After passing Bodie Island Light Station about 10 miles south of the park entrance on NC 12, continue approximately 45 miles to the town limits of Buxton. Within 1/2 mile turn left into the entrance of the light station. A visitors center is located temporarily in a double trailer at the four-way stop. The light station is in Phase II of the relocation project with ongoing improvements to the grounds and visitors facilities.

- There are various numbers assigned to the height of this lighthouse. Generally, the height is stated as 198 feet. After relocation, it gained about two feet in elevation.
- Cape Hatteras is the tallest brick lighthouse in North America.
- The lighthouse was completed in 1870.
- In 1870, with 24 panels in its 1st order Fresnel lens, the light turned at 1/4 RPM. Today, its modern aerobeacon emits a white "flash" every 7.5 seconds for eight "flashes" per minute.
- The beacon reaches 19 nautical miles; one nautical mile equals 1.15 statute miles.
- The last Keeper was Unaka Jennette who closed the lighthouse due to erosion in 1936. The light was housed in a skeletal tower in Buxton Woods until relighting the striped tower in 1950.
- The 1803, brown sandstone tower was destroyed after its Fresnel lens was shipped to Pigeon Point Light Station in California, following the completion of the 1870 tower.
- There are 268 cast-iron steps that lead to the lantern room.

The Cape Hatteras Lighthouse

HATTERAS BEACON LIGHT

(Lost Light- established 1855)

This tough little light known as the Hatteras Beacon Light was established in 1855 on Cape Point located about one and one half miles to the south of the Cape Hatteras Light Station. The beacon light guided coasting (local boats) until around 1906. It marked the turning point on a route from the Atlantic Ocean to the Pamlico Sound through a channel that served as a shortcut from Diamond Shoals. Its 6th order Fresnel lens was tended by the Third Assistant Keeper under the supervision of the Principal Keeper at the primary light station at Cape Hatteras, though the Beacon's Keeper was required to provide his own housing.

The beacon light was a wooden frame building that was painted red, and it exhibited a fixed white light twenty-five feet above mean (average) high water. In the beacon light's one-half century of service it was rebuilt and moved in 1857 due to erosion, moved 500 feet inland in 1858, darkened by Confederates in 1861, discontinued in 1879 due to erosion, re-established in 1883, and then moved another 200 feet inland in 1890. Around the turn of the century, the Lighthouse Service moved the light to a post nearby because erosion untiringly dogged the Hatteras Beacon Light each time it was relocated inland. The light was discontinued some time around 1906, and the Third Assistant Keeper's position ended at the Cape Hatteras Light Station.

The Hatteras Beacon Light was moved three times because of erosion. Situated on Cape Point, the light was always vulnerable to nor'easters (winter storms), tropical hurricanes, and erosion from wind and wave action. The entire structure was painted red and exhibited a fixed white light from a 6th order Fresnel lens for local maritime traffic. In the 1890s, the beacon was again painted, this time with a white frame, brown or red iron pilings, and a black lantern. The Hatteras Beacon Light witnessed the completion of a new tower at Cape Hatteras in 1870, and the subsequent destruction of the 1803 tower, and the painting of Hatteras's famous black and white spirals in 1873.

This photo is by U.S. Lighthouse Service photographer H. Bamber in the 1890s. It appears Bamber has captured the beacon when it had been spit polished with new shades of red on its frame.
Photo courtesy the Outer Banks History Center.

KEEPER WESLEY AUSTIN SAVES THE HATTERAS BEACON LIGHT

M. Wesley Austin, born 1864, worked his entire career for the U.S. Lighthouse Service. His formative years were spent aboard windjammers traveling the East Coast, and he entered the United States Lighthouse Service as a novice on tenders delivering staples to lighthouses. Austin's career spanned over four decades as Keeper at Cape Hatteras, Currituck Beach, and Ocracoke Light Stations from 1885-1929.

Austin's first assignment at a lighthouse began in 1885 as Third Assistant Keeper at $400 per annum. Under the supervision of the Principal Keeper at the Cape Hatteras Light Station, Austin tended the Hatteras Beacon Light. Though he was considered part of the Cape Hatteras staff, he had to provide his own housing. The beacon light was located to the south near the tip of Cape Point and the extremity of this location rendered it vulnerable to the wild Atlantic storms, especially dreaded hurricanes.

During one hurricane, gales had tipped the square wooden, cupola-topped tower about forty-five degrees shoreward. Only the bravery of Third Assistant Keeper Austin kept the light going.

In Austin's obituary, July 13, 1941, the story is told. The account reads, "...Often during his [Austin's] later years he tells about 'the night that he fought a hurricane and sweeping breakers to gain a foothold on this old beacon - how, while applying a flame to the oil wick, the old beacon soon to be abandoned, gave a lurch and toppled over to a 45 degree angle.' With a prayer on his lips, this man of great faith, clung to the leaning structure, lighted and adjusted the lamp so that its beam of light might warn mariners of the dangerous sand bar nearby. An unselfish prayer was his." His exemplary conduct distinguished Austin as a dedicated Keeper early in his career.

Later in his Lighthouse Service career in 1912, Wesley Austin and his wife, Belle Barnett, took five of their eight children from the Currituck Beach Light Station to the Ocracoke Light Station (the three older girls had married and stayed in Corolla), where Austin assumed his duties as Principal Keeper. He served in this respected role until his retirement in 1929.

OCRACOKE LIGHT STATION

Shell Castle Island Light (circa 1798)
Ocracoke Light 1823

The Ocracoke Lighthouse has long been a mecca for lighthouse enthusiasts. It is the second longest continuously operating lighthouse on the East Coast.

Ocracoke is currently the oldest operating light in North Carolina, and the second oldest continuously operating light on the East Coast. It sits on two picturesque acres in the heart of quaint Ocracoke village. The white conical tower rests quietly at the end of a picket fence with one side of the lighthouse more steeply sloped than the other, and a lantern room that is off-center. These irregularities only add to its historic character.

An earlier lighthouse site lay on the south side of Ocracoke Inlet on "Old Rock Island," one of the five islets west of Ocracoke Inlet. It became known in the late eighteenth century as "Shell Castle Island." Built by Henry Dearborn, the lighthouse is reported to have been lighted in 1798. Lightning destroyed the Shell Castle Island Light and its Keepers Quarters. And, as sand commonly shifts on the Outer Banks, the inlet changed away from Shell Castle Island and toward Ocracoke Island, which was chosen as the site for a new lighthouse.

The Ocracoke Lighthouse was completed in 1823 by Noah Porter of Massachusetts, and has shown continuously except for a period during the Civil War. Confederates removed its Fresnel lens so the light could not aid the Union Navy in its blockade of the southern coast. A replacement 4th order lens restored the light in 1864.

Ocracoke was once prized as the nearest harbor to Cape Hatteras; however, the inlet was difficult to navigate, and local pilots were regularly hired to steer vessels in and out. By mid-nineteenth century, Ocracoke Inlet ceased to be a major port and the lighthouse served as a guide for local coasting vessels.

Now, part of the Cape Hatteras National Seashore, this humble lighthouse is a favorite of many visitors to the Outer Banks.

 Quick Notes...

From the southern tip of Hatteras Island, take the car/passenger state operated ferry to Ocracoke Island (about forty minutes across). From the ferry dock on Ocracoke Island, drive about 12 miles south to the village on NC 12. Turn left onto Lighthouse Road in the village, continue until you see a small parking lot in front of lighthouse. Please be considerate of the neighboring private residences.

- Lighthouse information can be obtained at National Park Service visitors center near the Ocracoke-Cedar Island ferry dock.
- Diagonal astragals, an old lighthouse architectural style, form the distinguished pattern of its windows.
- The 1823 Ocracoke tower is currently the oldest operating lighthouse on NC coast. (Bald Head is five years older but no longer an active aid to navigation).
- The tower is 65 feet tall, and it is 75 feet to focal plane at the center of the lens.
- It has a fixed white light from a 4th order Fresnel lens.
- Keepers once boiled a concoction of glue and rice in huge vats and quickly applied the hot mixture as a protective coating to the brick.

Silver Lake provides an idyllic setting for Ocracoke village. Mariners have been coming here since the first English explorers wrecked nearby in 1585. Though once a busy shipping area, Ocracoke now is a favorite place for visitors who love sailing, shopping, or lighthouse viewing. The village harbors the Ocracoke Preservation Society Museum and a visitors center for the National Park Service, which now owns the Ocracoke Light Station.
Photo by Mark Riddick, New Light Photography.

CAPE LOOKOUT LIGHT STATION

(First tower 1812 and second tower 1859)

At Cape Lookout, the North Carolina shoreline takes a dramatic westerly swing, rendering it a dangerous harbinger of shoaling sand called Lookout Shoals, much like the dreaded Diamond Shoals at Cape Hatteras and Frying Pan Shoals of the Cape Fear area. Extending from these capes are sand bars and large deposits of sand which shoal, or pile up, and create shallow waters for miles into the Atlantic Ocean. These fingers of shifting sand have stopped scores of ships dead in their tracks.

An 1806 report to Congress states, "It is supposed there i no part of the American Coast where vessels are more exposed to shipwreck, than they are in passing along the shores of North Carolina, in the neighborhood of those shoals."

To warn ships of these dangers around Lookout Shoals, lighthouse was built in 1812, and its first Keeper was William Fulford.

A description of the early lighthouse appears in an 1817 report written by Winslow Lewis, designer of the lamp system used in virtually every American lighthouse. Lewis wrote the original light list produced in this country for the U.S. Lighthouse Establishment and described the tower, "1817 Situated on Cape Look Out [sic], on the coast of North Carolina The Lantern is 95 feet above the sea, and contains a fixed light This light can be seen without the shoals, which extend out from it; But vessels passing them in the night, ought rather to trust to the lead than the light. The light-house is painted in horizontal stripes, alternately red and white, and appears at a distance like a ship of war with her sails clewed up, and was often taken for such during the late war."

Like the 1803 tower at Hatteras, the first Cape Lookout Lighthouse utilized a collection of Argand oil burning lamps with parabolic reflectors to get the light out beyond the shoals But Lewis himself witnesses his system's insufficiency in the report quoted above. He told ship captains to check the depth in fathoms ("trust to the lead," a piece of metal attached to a thin rope and dropped over the side to measure water depth) rather than rely on the light. Lookout Shoals, always in a state of flux, could suddenly reduce the water's depth to four feet or less at low tide, and a mariner could run across the shoals before seeing the beacon's warning.

Sailors criticized the Lewis lighting system for decades, and finally, by the late 1840s, there was a strong voice for putting Fresnel lenses in America's towers. Though more expensive at $6,500 in 1850, the savings in fuel in the long run would pay for the investment.

Overdue improvement came in 1854. A 1st order Fresnel lens from France was installed in Cape Lookout; it was a cathedral-shaped, lens, almost a dozen feet high, with a metal frame that held dazzling crown glass prisms. When an oil lamp was placed in the center of the lens, the prisms gathered up every candela of light and condensed them into a beam that streamed out into the darkness around Cape Lookout. This brilliant nightlight was complemented by the tower's red and white horizontal stripes as a daymark. However, the mariner still had trouble seeing the light in time to avoid Lookout Shoals.

As a new approach to improve the tower, Lighthouse Service officials ordered a new tower at Cape Lookout, one taller than any lighthouse in the country. Completed in 1859, it stood 165 feet with eight-foot-thick, double brick walls, one inside the other, which tapered to two feet at the top. It was this tower, which still stands today, that became the model for the

Above: The Cape Lookout Lighthouse wears its unique daymark of vivid black and white checkers, called "diamonds" today.

Below: The Cape Lookout Light Station was photographed by U.S. Lighthouse Service photographer H. Bamber in the 1890s. This particular print was found in a trunk purchased in an estate auction in New England. *From the author's personal collection.*

Above: The Cape Lookout Lighthouse as seen from Core Sound appears in splendor on New Years Day 2000. A new century at Cape Lookout begins.

all North Carolina coastal lights built after the Civil War - Cape Hatteras, Bodie Island, and Currituck Beach. Other southern lights would be designed after this successful lighthouse model including Morris Island, South Carolina, and St. Augustine, Florida.

However, this new lighthouse had a rough beginning because not long after the new tower had been built, the Civil War began. In 1861, the Confederate Light House Bureau assumed control of all southern lighthouses, including those in North Carolina. Orders were issued to darken coastal lights, dis-assemble the Fresnel lenses, and move them inland away from possible capture by Union forces threatening to dominate the coast.

Confederate control of the coast was short-lived because Union troops captured Beaufort and Cape Lookout in 1862, regaining control of the North Carolina lighthouses for the Light-House Board. In 1863, a 3rd order Fresnel lens replaced the stolen one at Cape Lookout and reactivated the new tower; this relighting proved temporary.

In April of 1864, a small group of Confederate commandos, with the aid of Confederate spies, including a beautiful young woman, were able to slip through Union lines, blow up the 1812 tower, and render serious damage to the new one. Defective gun powder saved the 1859 tower from ruin; howev-er, the blast destroyed the 3rd order Fresnel lens, causing an additional request to Lighthouse Service headquarters in D.C. for another Fresnel lens. Reactivated, the lighthouse continued service permanently.

To improve the warning to mariners about the ever-chang-ing Lookout Shoals, a lightship was placed near the outer edge of the shoals in 1903. It remained in service until 1933 when its radio beacon and electric lighting equipment were salvaged and installed in the lighthouse.

In 1939 the Bureau of Lighthouses was incorporated into the U.S. Coast Guard, and the grand era of civilian lighthouse Keepers and their families who kept the lights burning on America's shores came to a close. Automation of the lights would continue until manned lights were history. Cape Lookout

became automated in 1950.

President Lyndon B. Johnson authorized the Cape Lookout National Seashore in 1966, which includes the lighthouse and Portsmouth Village. The U.S. Coast Guard still owns and main-tains the lighthouse as an active aid to navigation. The modern aerobeacon emits a flash of white light every 15 seconds. Although the tower is closed to the public, the Double Keepers Quarters nearby is open as a National Park Service visitors cen-ter with lighthouse exhibits sponsored by the Outer Banks Lighthouse Society.

Cape Lookout has historical importance as the first tall, coastal lighthouse in North Carolina and on the East Coast. To preserve it as an icon of our maritime history, it needs complete renovation. Failing ironwork and crumbling brick from moisture trapped within the tower threaten to destroy this beautiful lighthouse.

 Quick Notes...

Directions: From Morehead City follow U.S. 70 through Beaufort to Otway. Turn towards Harkers Island and follow signs to Cape Lookout National Seashore headquarters at the end of the island. On the way, you will see several private passenger ferries that provide service to the lighthouse locat-ed on Core Banks Island, about a 20-minute boat ride (take your own food and water). While in the area, be sure to see the N.C. Maritime Museum on the Beaufort waterfront.

- Two towers have been on this site: 1812 and 1859.
- The existing Keepers Quarters was built in 1873, and mineral oil (kerosene) replaced the use of whale oil.
- The 1859 tower served as the architectural model for the lights at Cape Hatteras, Bodie Island, and Currituck Beach.
- The height of the present tower is 165 feet.
- The modern optic is an aerobeacon that gives 1 white flash every 15 seconds, reaching out 19 nautical miles.
- Two women served as Keepers: Charlotte Ann Mason Moore 1872-75 as First Assistant to her father, Maneon W. Mason, and Emily Julia Mason, Principal Keeper 1876-78, when she replaced her father as Keeper.

THE LOST LIGHTS OF NORTH CAROLINA
Once They Sparkled Like Diamonds on the Rivers and Sounds

A lighthouse tender brings supplies to Pamlico Point Lighthouse at the mouth of the Pamlico River. Photo is circa 1890s. Tenders brought coal, wood, and maintenance supplies, perhaps new lamp wicks or paint, to all the lighthouses. Note the Lighthouse Service insignia on the captain's cap. Sometimes the Lighthouse Inspector was on board to make sure Keepers were doing their duties according to strict Lighthouse Service regulations. The Pamlico Point Light had a fog bell, which can be seen at the top right of the building. These sound lights were in shallow water, but often they were miles from signs of civilization including a post office, general store, or medical help. A Keeper's only transportation was a boat, often his own.

Imagine driving along the interstate highway system without signs marking your entrances and exits for destinations. You can then imagine what it was like navigating the sounds and rivers of North Carolina before the United States Lighthouse Service built the inland lights in the 19th century. By 1891, each evening, the lamps' flames were afire inside their Fresnel lenses. These lights marked the turns for the Neuse, New, Pamlico, Roanoke, and Pasquotank Rivers. Once guided only by stars that were light-years away, mariners had gained something tangible to follow. The river and sound lights gave nocturnal hitchhikers of current and wind a way to turn a paradox into the familiar.

From the Cape Fear River to the Currituck Sound, navigators watched for these estuarine lighthouses as today's drivers watch for green interstate exit signs. Like mile markers, the Croatan and Roanoke Marshes Lights identified the north and south entrances of a channel through the Croatan Sound linking the Albemarle and Pamlico Sounds. Veteran watermen have witnessed the immense comfort in spotting one of these lighthouses in fair weather and foul. No amount of value can be placed on lights that brought many fishermen and travelers home safely instead of their wandering the rivers and sounds during darkness, fog, and storm. In the days before radio, "seeing was believing."

Today, however, visual reminders of these old lighthouses are rare. Along the Cape Fear River, the remains of Price's Creek Light can be seen from the Ft. Fisher - Southport Ferry. It is the only river or sound light left in its original location, and the land upon which it rests is privately owned. Of the few river and sound lights that the U.S. Coast Guard sold for a small fee, the only survivor is the Roanoke River Light, which was moved to Edenton in 1955 and became a private residence. All the others are gone.

A typical North Carolina sound or river light, commonly called a "screw-pile light," was a white, two-storied, four-sided house with a black iron lantern room mounted on the roof. Tight quarters afforded about 1,000 square feet of work/living/play area, all in one. The lighthouse was about twelve feet above the water and was supported by iron pilings usually painted red or black, with the Keeper's boat kept in dry-dock at the first floor level. A fog bell hung under the roof or outside a dormer over the first floor while a platform under the building served as storage for various supplies; every inch of space was used. Two Keepers manned each lighthouse and took their skiff to fetch groceries or medical help from miles away.

A century ago, getting on a boat and traveling from Elizabeth City to Nags Head was as easy as getting in your car. River and sound traffic followed green and red channel markers like the white and yellow lines of today's highways. Boaters read the lighthouses' positions as signposts to the bustling ports of Elizabeth City, Washington, New Bern, Beaufort, and Wilmington. Occasionally, travelers saluted lighthouse Keepers, stopping to chat, to share a fresh fish, or to bring news from the mainland.

Abandoned and forgotten, these structures were once an important part of our aquatic highway system and our maritime history. The following lists of the lights that once existed on North Carolina's sounds and rivers, include their predecessors, light vessels.

From the light lists of the U.S. Lighthouse Service, *List of Light-Houses, lighted-beacons, and floating lights of the United States by the Light-House Board,* the following statistics are given about the river lights and lightships. Due to inconsistent reports, dates given by these reports may be approximate.

Three main routes needed in the busy sounds were first marked by light-vessels beginning in the 1820s: Pamlico to Core Sound; the Neuse River into Pamlico Sound and west into the Pamlico River; and finally, through Albemarle Sound into the Pasquotank River.

Light-vessels suffered the same fate as all N.C. lights during the Civil War. Lights were either stolen or the structure was severely damaged or destroyed. By the end of the war, replacement of all lightships of the inland waters had begun.

Wade's Point Light-Vessel 1845
Roanoke Island or Croatan Light-Vessel 1835
Long Shoal Light-Vessel 1825
Nine-Foot Shoal Light-Vessel 1827 northwest of Ocracoke
Brant Island Shoal Light-Vessel 1831 southern Pamlico Sound
Neuse River Light-Vessel 1828 northern entrance to Neuse River
Harbor Island Light-Vessel 1836 between Pamlico and Core Sound
Roanoke River Light-Vessel 1835
Horseshoe Shoal Light-Vessel 1851 between New Inlet and Price's Creek
Royal Shoal Light-Vessel 1825 on southwest point, 2 miles from the Ocracoke Light, meant to mark Ocracoke Inlet into Pamlico Sound and points beyond; replaced by river light 1867
Harkers Island Light-Vessel 1836, on Harbor Island bar, between Pamlico and Core Sounds
Ocracoke Channel Light-Vessel 1852, teamed up as a range light for a few years with a light on a Keeper's house on "Beacon's Island" to guide boats into the channel until the channel closed.

Light-vessels were gradually replaced by screwpiles and range lights with some lights discontinued after the Civil War and many new lights established. In general north-south order, here is a list of these river and sound lights:
North River 1866
Wade's Point badly burned in Civil War, repaired 1866, rebuilt 1899, guide from north side of Albemarle Sound into Pasquotank River
Roanoke River 1866
Laurel Point (Albemarle Sound) 1880
Croatan (a.k.a Roanoke Island or Mashoes Creek) 1860; destroyed in Civil War; rebuilt 1866
Roanoke Marshes reported as early as 1830 with 10 lamps; rebuilt 1857; rebuilt 1877; a compressed-air siren fog signal installed
Long Shoal 1867
Gull Shoal (west side of Pamlico Sound) 1891
Pamlico Point (east side of the shoal marking out from Pamlico Pt. south side entrance to Pamlico River) reported as early as 1828; "refitted" 1867; rebuilt 1891

At right is the Roanoke Marshes Lighthouse, rebuilt in 1877. More than mere markers akin to our highway signs today, these lighthouses were also homes to Keepers and their visiting families. In a time when coastal towns were isolated and water travel could be solitary, these modest beacons gave assurance to the traveler that he was not alone.

Neuse River (at mouth of) 1862
N.W. Point Royal Shoal 1857
S.W. Point Royal Shoal 1867, discontinued 1880; relit 1887
Shell Castle Island 1798 (see Ocracoke p 13)
Beacon Island 1853-57 discontinued (light on Keeper's house as range with Ocracoke light-vessel in the channel)
Hatteras Inlet (a.k.a. Oliver's Reef) 1874
Hatteras Beacon 1855 (see page 12)
Brant Island Shoal 1851; rebuilt 1877
Harbor Island 1867; discontinued 1880; relit 1888, guide into Core Sound
Bogue Banks (Beaufort Inlet at Ft. Macon) 1855 range lights; one in front of fort, the second to rear, 4th and 5th order lenses)

Lights of Cape Fear
Cape Fear (see Bald Head Light p. 17)
Orton's Plantation 1849 west bank of Cape Fear at Orton's Plantation; darkened in Civil War, not relit
Campbell's Island 1849 middle of northern Cape Fear; darkened in Civil War, not relit
Federal Point 1866 (earlier light described in 1816 with 8 lamps and rebuilt 1836) on east bank of Cape Fear at Ft. Fisher
Horseshoe Shoal 1868 at mouth of New River, between New Inlet and Price's Creek
Price's Creek (see Prices' Creek p. 16) west bank of Cape Fear near Southport
Oak Island Range Lights 1849; originally two brick towers, later frame; range lights for crossing Oak Island bar
Upper Jetty Range 1855, northern Cape Fear, led to port of Wilmington

The large light vessels stationed at sea:
Frying-Pan Shoals Light-Vessel 1854; removed in Civil War; replaced 1865; replaced again 1966 by "Texas Tower" which is now automated
Lookout Shoals Light-Vessel 1903-1933
Diamond Shoals Lightship 1824 until 1827 when blown off station; not replaced until 1897; destroyed by German U-boat 1918; replaced and remained on station until replaced by "Texas Tower" 1967; automated 1977

BALD HEAD (OLD BALDY) LIGHTHOUSE

Lost first tower 1794, second (standing) tower 1818
Destroyed third skeleton tower (Cape Fear)1903

Bald Head Lighthouse, the oldest standing tower in North Carolina, greet the visitor with a stone plaque over the door boldly stating AD 1817, the yea the site was established, and the light was activated in 1818. One can immed ately see and feel the history lingering. Its octagonal exterior depicts the earl era of lighthouse architectural style in America. Its ancient look in mottle tones of rough plaster evokes the familiar identity it carries today as "Ol Baldy."

Yet, there was earlier lighthouse history that began near this site. The firs Bald Head Light was constructed in 1794 with funds partially provided by th North Carolina General Assembly enacted in 1784. A duty levied on cargo ca ried along the Cape Fear River yielded money earmarked for lighthouse con struction on Smith Island, also known as Bald Head Island. Mr. Smith, th island's owner, granted 19 acres in 1790. When the nation's government too over responsibility for lighthouse construction, it ordered the first Bald Hea Light to be built on the river. Erosion took care of this light; the Cape Fear Rive has drowned prestigious boat pilots, mariners, and a light station.

In summary, the warning light of the Bald Head Island area has bee passed from tower to tower. The first light (1795) was built on the riverbank and gave way to the present Old Baldy tower. The second, existing tower wa completed in 1818 on the southwest bank at the main entrance to the Cap Fear River. Old Baldy was decommissioned when the second light at Feder. Point took up position at the north entrance to the river in 1866. Subsequentl the New Inlet closed due to shoaling, and Federal Point was deactivated i 1880. This put Old Baldy back in action, and it remained an active aid to nav gation until the lighthouse was deactivated in 1935 for the last time.

At the turn of the twentieth century, a significant change had occurred i the channel through the Cape Fear River, and a coastal light was needec Therefore, the Bureau of Lighthouses constructed an iron skeleton tower i 1903 at the end of Federal Road on the southeast tip of Smith Island. Its onl Keeper, Charlie Swan, manned the tower until the government destroyed it b dynamite blasts in 1958. The torch was passed to the modern Oak Islan Lighthouse on a neighboring island.

Today, the Bald Head Lighthouse is listed on the National Register of Histori Places. It is cared for by the Old Baldy Foundation, a nonprofit organizatio that restored the tower and reopened it to the public for climbing in 1995.

The Old Baldy Foundation completed a reproduction of the 1850 Keepers Quarters near the tower and invites the public to experience th interpretation of life on Smith Island in that era. A gift shop is also housed wit in the Keepers Quarters/museum.

Above: The 1818 Bald Head Lighthouse rises above the trees that now grow at its base. It is the oldest lighthouse in North Carolina and it is also known affectionately as "Old Baldy."

Below: A view of the front face of this historic tower exhibits its old octagonal design. Lighthouses were improved with conical towers to lessen resistance to lashing winds and storm-driven rain. A plaque records the date of the site's establishment in 1817. The tower was completed in 1818.

 Quick Notes...

Directions: Bald Head Island can be reached only by passenger ferry from Southport. In Southport, turn west off NC 211 onto West 9th Street and follow signs to the ferry dock on Indigo Plantation grounds. Ferry information (910) 457-5003

- Old Baldy is the second of three towers built on Bald Head Island to aid mariners navigating the Cape Fear River to and from the deep water port of Wilmington, N.C.
- While in the area visit Fort Fisher, built on the site of Federal Point, location of three destroyed lights, now a state historic site with a museum.
- Old Baldy Foundation has built a reproduction of the 1850s Keeper's Cottage as a museum near the tower in the grove of old live oaks.
- For more information: Old Baldy Foundation, Inc. P.O. Box 3007 Bald Head Island, NC 28461 or (910) 457-7481

OAK ISLAND LIGHT STATION

Established 1958

In 1958, nineteen years after the U.S. Coast Guard assumed responsibility or America's aids to navigation, a 155-foot, commanding lighthouse was completed in Caswell Beach on Oak Island. Using twentieth century engineering knowledge, the tower was built by pouring reinforced concrete into a tall, cylindrical mold, one section at a time. The lantern room is aluminum and holds eight, high-intensity, 480-volt mercury arc bulbs, which normally flash 1.4 million candlepower. When bad weather renders visibility of the light below 19 nautical miles, its beam can be increased to 14 million candlepower. So intense is the heat from this light that protective clothing must be worn while doing maintenance in the lantern room.

Bald Head Lighthouse represents one bookend to the volumes of U.S. Lighthouse Service construction annals. Built by the U.S. Coast Guard, Oak Island Lighthouse and its contemporary on Sullivan's Island in South Carolina serve as the other. Oak Island Lighthouse has historical importance as one of the last two lighthouses ever built in the United States.

 Quick Notes...

In Southport on NC 211, take 133 south. Continue to the end of 133 and turn left onto a paved road to Caswell Beach. The lighthouse will be on the left side of road. It is not open to the public, but there are good views from the highway.

- This beacon uses modern technology, including a lantern room made of lightweight aluminum, and powerful mercury arc bulbs, which may be intensified during fog up to fourteen million candlepower.
- Its foundation is driven deep into the subsurface bedrock 125 feet.
- There are 134 steps to the lantern gallery.
- The lighthouse is meant to be flexible, built to sway three feet in gale-force winds.

PRICE'S CREEK LIGHTHOUSE

(Ruins - established 1850)

The ruins of this pre-Civil War lighthouse is all that remains of a series of range lights that were built to guide ships through a channel in the Cape Fear River to the port of Wilmington. Located on the west bank of the Cape Fear River, near Price's Creek, this front range light displayed a fixed white light from a 6th order Fresnel lens. The rear range light was also a fixed white light of the 6th order on the Keeper's dwelling, which is now gone. By lining up the two lights, with the higher light directly over the lower light, a mariner could determine where the channel turned for that part of the river.

During the Civil War, the Confederate Light House Bureau took over the operation of these river lights for blockade runners. Boats supporting the Rebel cause could navigate the river at night to take cotton to Bermuda (where it was shipped to England) and return with necessities for the Confederate armies. As the Union took control of coastal North Carolina, the Confederates damaged or destroyed as many lighthouses as possible. Price's Creek is an example of one of these damaged lights that was not re-established after the war.

 Quick Notes...

The ruins of this light can be best viewed from the Fort Fisher-Southport Ferry.

- The ruins of Price's Creek Light are located on the south bank of the Cape Fear River near Southport on commercial property; it is not accessible to the public.
- Its has significant historical importance as the last remaining river light on the Cape Fear River.
- Originally, Price's Creek was a front range light with a rear range light above and behind it on the Keepers Quarters. By lining up the two lights, one over the other, a ship's captain recognized the entrance to a section of a channel leading through the Cape Fear River to and from the port of Wilmington.

*The sands have sifted through the hourglass. The time for
fond farewell draws near.*

*I walk away from my window, the wilds before me indelibly
etched within.*

Again I hear the mighty ocean roar.
Come back. Come back.
I will remember.
I have danced with the angels in my time beside the sea.

Randy Taylor

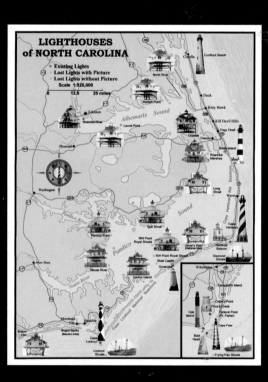

BEAUTIFUL COLOR PHOTOGRAPHS
Map of 20 lighthouse locations in North Carolina
Interesting histories of major lighthouses

For centuries, mariners traveling the East Coast of the United States have dreaded the North Carolina coastline, better known as the "Graveyard of the Atlantic." The shores here offered up treacherous Cape Fear, the "Promontorium Tremendum" of Cape Lookout, dreaded Diamond Shoals of Cape Hatteras, and the featureless sand beaches along Bodie Island and Currituck with their unpredictable shoals lurking under the waves. For almost 200 years these storied sentinels have lighted the night and beamed a warning to sailors.

Read about these proud beacons including the lost lights of the rivers and sounds of North Carolina. Within this well-researched booklet you will find a unique map, beautiful color photographs, intriguing facts and directions to the North Carolina Lighthouses.

Lighthouse Publications   P.O. Box 1124   Morehead City, NC 28557

ISBN 0-9676537-1-1 $4.95

T1-BIV-059

Grammar Sense 2A

WORKBOOK

...well

OXFORD